PINK

——————

A SHORT UNAUTHORIZED BIOGRAPHY

FAMELIFE BIOS

1

WHO IS PINK

Pink is an American singer-songwriter who has dabbled in acting and has been active in her endeavors. She was born for singing and songwriting, and as a child, she started writing songs with grave implications. Her career began when she joined as a vocalist and dancer when she was 14 years old, and she hasn't stopped since. Despite her tough-girl persona, she exposed her softer side to the public and has endorsed various causes. She is a vocal spokesperson for the LGBTQ community and better animal care, lending her celebrity to campaigns run by People for the Ethical Treatment of Animals (PETA) (PETA). She also reached out to charities and donated a considerable amount of money to the Human Rights Campaign, UNICEF, and Save the Children.

PINK WAS BORN on September 8, 1979, in Doylestown, Pennsylvania. Pink Moore was Jim and Judy Moore's second child. In a suburb of Doylestown, Pennsylvania, she lived a relatively everyday middle-class life. Pink's parents divorced when she was three years old due to their strained relationship. Pink'sIn part, Pink's rebellious mentality was ignited by their breakup and eventual dissolution of their marriage. She never discussed what went wrong or understood how it influenced her until several years later. Pink started acting out after just a few years. Despite having asthma, she started smoking at nine and continued for several years. Pink had her first tattoo and tongue piercing when she was 12 years old. On the other hand, Pink found solace in music as early as the age of 13.

PINK GOT her name from the film Reservoir Dogs, which she saw as a teenager whose character Mr. Pink was someone her friends all decided she looked like. Pink spent several years in Philadelphia's club scene, singing guest spots and appearing on talent shows. A local DJ asked her to sing backup for his rap party, Schools of Thought, when she was 13 years old. Soon after, she was noticed by a record executive and joined a female R&B group called choice. She became independent and went solo when she decided to sign with LaFace Records after the female group didn't work out. Her debut album entitled Can't Take Me Anywhere was launched in 2000. Pink also co-wrote several of her songs for the album, which went multi-platinum by the end of the year. Her first single, "There You Go," was a Top 10 success and was certified gold. P! nk gradually moved away from her early R&B style from 2001's quintuple-platinum M! ssundaztood to 2003's Grammy-winning Try This, collaborating with her composers Linda Perry, Tim Armstrong (Rancid), and Butch Walker that gave her this iconic rousing pop music with a distinct rock edge. After being nominated for over a dozen Grammy Awards, she was awarded Best Pop Collaboration in 2002, which made to Lady Marmalade's cover and won for her song Trouble in the Year 2004 as the Best Female Rock Vocal Performance. In 2016, she got an Emmy for "Today's the Day," the Ellen DeGeneres Show theme. Hurts 2B Human was released in 2019, and it, like her previous two albums, topped the Billboard 200.

Pink has established herself as a pop culture icon. She was the first non-British artist to garner the Brit Award for Outstanding Contribution to British music in 2019 and the first non-British artist to be awarded since the Brit Awards started in 1977. This experience was extra special for her as she was chosen ahead of British musician Phil Collins, who had been in the career for so long and sold numerous albums but has never won the award. Pink, known for her raspy voice and acrobatic stage presence, has sold over 90 million albums worldwide as of 2020, making her one of the world's most successful musicians. She earned three Grammy Awards followed by two Brit Awards. She was ranked tenth on VH1's list of the 100 Greatest Women in Music, and she gained the label as the Woman of the Year by Billboard in 2013. She received the BMI President's Award for "outstanding achievement in songwriting and global impact on pop music and the entertainment industry." With a string of number one hits and millions of albums sold worldwide, P!nk is cited as one of the world's most commercially successful pop stars.

THINGS PEOPLE HAVE SAID ABOUT PINK

"Pink stood up for her songs, cracked the music industry's mold, and scored a breakthrough hit," writes Robert Hilburn of the Los Angeles Times, "challenging a school of teen singers to find their sounds as well." "[Pink] also began a race among other teen pop stars, such as Christina Aguilera, to add substance to their sound," he continues. Ann Powers calls her a "powerhouse vocalist," claiming that her combination of defiance, emotional rawness, humor, and "infectious" dance beats made her "a blueprint for the mashup approach of latter-day divas like Katy Perry, Kesha, and Rihanna." Rolling Stone's Rob Sheffield had this to say: "People, I believe, react to her sense of freedom and commitment. It motivates people as this is a prolific pop artist who is often well-known and profitable, and other times unknown, but who never stops creating her brand of music." "A deceptively good singer... who can out-sing almost everyone," says MTV's James Montgomery. She has the ability to out-crazy Lady Gaga and Lily. She's the complete pop-star bundle, with all the qualities you'd look for in a performer, entertainer, or icon. Despite all of these issues circulating her, that didn't stop her from reaching her dream. "Breaking boundaries comes at a cost." Her voice is described as "prodigious" by The Guardian. "A powerhouse vocalist," according to Ann Powers of the Los Angeles Times. Pink's "raw," "soulful" voice and ability to emote have also been praised. Her voice was described as "husky" and "gutsy" by The Philadelphia Inquirer, who also praised her for maturing into a "powerfully emotive vocalist" and compared her to Janis Joplin. I'd never heard anyone sing like that life before, even though I was in the audience. Her voice struck me like a sledgehammer, and I felt like I was in a wind tunnel. It was fantastic."

Kelly Clarkson calls her "one of the most underrated vocals capable of singing anything, from rock and pop to folk and R&B," describing her as having "one of the most underrated vocals capable of singing anything, from rock and pop to folk and R&B."

3

PINK IS BORN

Pink was born On September 8, 1979. Alecia Beth Moore, popularly known as Pink, was born in Doylestown, Pennsylvania, the second child of Jim and Judy Moore. She lived a fairly typical middle-class life in Doylestown, Pennsylvania. Her mother works as an emergency nurse, and an insurance company employed her father. Despite being a healthy baby at birth, she developed asthma early in life, which troubled her for the rest of her life. Her parents' marital troubles started when she was a toddler and eventually led to their divorce.

PINK ADMITTED that she didn't get along with her Solo Mom, Judith "Judy" Moore, for years, but now that she's an adult, she understands how difficult her mother's journey was. Following the divorce, Judith was left to care for her children independently. She was working full-time, going to her children's school full-time, and raising two troublemakers simultaneously. When Pink was 15, Judith kicked her daughter out of the house due to a conflict between mother and daughter. Through time, their connection grew, and now, Pink considered her one of her closest friends.

JIM MOORE, Pink's father, remained remarkably close to her and influenced her. He is one of those brave men who served during the Vietnam War and worked in the insurance industry. He taught her how to fight, use knives and weapons, and break wrists, among other things. He also inspired her when teaching her how to play the guitar and introduced her to Bob Dylan and Don McLean's music. It acted as a hidden track on the album and was opened by an introduction from Pink about the song's context in Pink's fourteenth and final track from her fourth studio album. I'm Not Dead. It was written in collaboration with her father, Jim Moore, who contributed most of the material. Jim acted as Pink's manager in addition to being her co-writer, making it a father-daughter bonding experience.

HER MOTHER CAME of Ashkenazi Jewish descent, and her father is of Irish, German, and English descent. Pink self-identifies as Jewish and describes herself as an "Irish-German-Lithuanian-Jew."

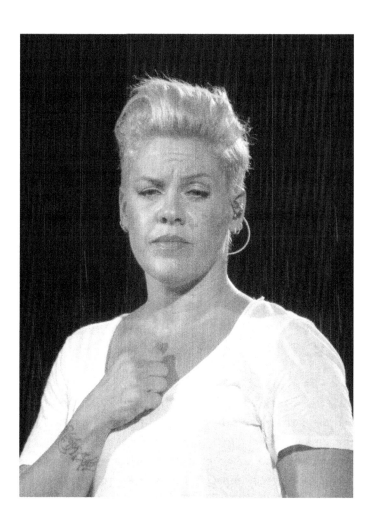

4

GROWING UP WITH PINK

In a suburb of Doylestown, Pennsylvania, she lived a relatively everyday middle-class life. Pink's parents divorced when she was three years old due to their strained relationship. In part, pink's rebellious mentality was ignited by their breakup and eventual dissolution of their marriage.

Despite being a healthy baby at birth, she developed asthma early in life, which troubled her for the rest of her life. Pink was trained to become a gymnast from ages four to twelve. She had never considered what went wrong or understood how it impacted her after her parents divorced when she was ten years old. Pink began acting poorly after just a few years. Despite having asthma, she started smoking at nine and continued for several years. Pink had her first tattoo and tongue piercing when she was 12 years old.

She had her high school years at 'Central Bucks High

School West,' and she was just a simple teenager with asthma. She was a regular worker in Philadelphia clubs by the early age of 13, first becoming a dancer, then as a backup singer for a popular local hip-hop group called Schoolz of Thought. Pink also stated that she grew up in a family with the same admiration for music. Even in her early days, she started to write her songs when she was 14 years old, and the same year, a local DJ at Club Fever began inviting her onstage every Friday to perform a song. Her mother was quoted as saying that her lyrics were "deep." She wrote lyrics that expressed her emotions.

PINK, who earned her nickname for her frequent blushing, continued to pursue her dream while working at fast-food restaurants and performing at Philadelphia hip-hop night-clubs, unfazed and armed with a strong singing voice. After a failed bid with another LaFace-signed R&B group, she remained with the label to record her first solo album, Can't Take Me Anywhere, at 19.

5

PINK'S PERSONAL RELATIONSHIPS

Pink was rumored to have had feelings for a rapper, a guitarist, and an NSYNC member long before that. In 2002, the singer was linked to the Naughty by Nature rapper. Every time he was asked about the rumors about their relationship, Treach placed an end to them. In 2003, Tommy and Pink were rumored to be dating, but their romance was never confirmed. When asked if Tommy was "having sex" with Pink on The Howard Stern Show in 2004, Tommy's ex Pamela Anderson said, "Oh yeah." Pink had an intimate friendship with Joey Fatone in the early 2000s. In the year 2013, there was an issue of Glamour. Pink announced her millennial romance with the *NSYNC star.

Pink's life was changing outside of the studio as well. After proposing to her boyfriend, Motocross star Carey Hart, she married him in Costa Rica during one of his races. As her parents ', Pink's marriage to Hart was turbulent, and the pair divorced only two years after they exchanged vows. Hart also starred in the video for her 2008 single "So What," about their breakup. During their separation, the pair pursued marital therapy in the hopes of reconciling. Her fifth album, Funhouse (2008), was inspired by the raw emotions resulting from her divorce. It became a commercial success, placing at No. 2 on the Billboard chart and launching a wild, worldwide tour in which she performs blindfolded and sings upside-down on a trapeze on many occasions.

PINK'S healing was aided by music, and her reflection on her deteriorating relationship with Hart helped the couple reunite. In an interview last February 2010 with Oprah Winfrey, Pink announced publicly that she and her husband were back to loving one another, which ended the rumors that circulated for months. She told Winfrey that her divorce from Hart gave her vital insights about herself and how to behave in a relationship properly. Their daughter Willow Sage was welcomed by the world last June of 2011. In December 2016, she delivered their second child, a healthy baby boy named Jameson Moon.

6

THE RISE OF PINK

Pink, on the other hand, had a solid musical talent. Pink started playing in clubs in Philadelphia when she was about 14 years old. At this point, she began using the stage name "Pink." She'd had that nickname for a long time at that point, and it had started as "a mean thing." She got her name from Quentin Tarantino's film Reservoir Dogs' character "Mr. Pink." ONE EVENING, an MCA executive encountered the sassy teen and invited her to audition for a new R&B group emerging. Pink was accepted into the party, which is known as Basic Instinct. Despite having a record contract and much studio time, the band never got off the ground. Basic Instinct was only together for two years before disbanding. LaFace Records gave pink a solo recording contract in 1995 after they saw her potential. Her debut studio album entitled Can't Take Me Home, which has an R&B feel, was a certified double-platinum in the United States, and two of her singles, entitled There You Go and Most Girls, were included in Billboard Hot 100 top-ten singles. With the collaboration single "Lady Marmalade" from the Moulin Rouge! The soundtrack gained even more fame, reaching the top of several charts worldwide. She returned her focus of sound to pop-rock in 2001, leading to her second studio album Missundaztood which has made more than 13 million copies worldwide and created international number-one singles.

PINK WON the category for Best Female Rock Vocal Performance in the Grammy's for her third studio album, Try This, released in 2003, even though it sold slightly less than her previous work. I'm Not Dead and Funhouse, her fourth and fifth studio albums, respectively, brought her back to the top of the charts, with the top-ten singles "Who Knew" and "U + Ur Hand," as well. As the number-one dollar "So What." Pink's sixth studio album, The Truth About Love (2012), debuted at number one on the Billboard 200 and produced her fourth US number-one single, "Just Give Me a Reason." In 2014, Pink released Rose Ave., a collaboration album with Canadian musician Dallas Green as part of the You+Me folk music duo.

PINK HAS STRENGTHENED her status as a cultural symbol. She was the first non-British artist to win the Brit Award for Outstanding Contribution to British music in 2019 and the first non-British artist to receive the award since the Brit Awards began in 1977. (The BPI Awards were formerly known as the BPI Awards). This was especially impressive as she was chosen ahead of British musician Phil Collins, who had been in the career for so long and sold numerous albums but has never won the award. Pink, known for her raspy voice and acrobatic stage presence, has sold over 90 million albums worldwide as of 2020, making her one of the world's most successful musicians. Three Grammy Awards, two Brit Awards, a Daytime Emmy Award, and seven MTV Video Music Awards, including the Michael Jackson Video Vanguard Award, are her many achievements. The singer was chosen as the Pop Songs Artist of the Decade by Billboard in 2009. Pink was also the second most-played female solo artist in the UK during the 2000s, behind Madonna. She was ranked tenth on VH1's list of the 100 Greatest Women in Music, and she was named Woman of the Year by Billboard in 2013. Because of her exceptional songwriting skills and providing a global impact on pop music and the entertainment industry, she received a BMI President's Award at the 63rd annual BMI Pop Awards.

7

SIGNIFICANT CAREER MILESTONES

Pink, who was never one to mask her true feelings, was dissatisfied despite her newfound popularity and success. Feeling overshadowed by the abundance of pretty singers that dominated the industry, Pink decided to pursue a more profound, edgier concept for her music. In London's Daily Mail, she stated that she wasted no blood, sweat, or tears on her first album. She added that there was no emotional exchange between her and the other musicians.

PINK, on the other hand, had a positive experience with both. Her talent was too obvious to ignore, and she went it alone with the help of LaFace, Choice's former label. After renewing her identity by changing her name from what her family brought Alecia Moore into Pink, she immediately started recording her first solo album, Can't Take Me Anywhere. The album was a surprise smash success when released in 2000, going double platinum and spawning two Top 10 singles: "There You Go" and "Most Girls." Her tour schedule, which saw her opening for the famous boy band *NSYNC, helped boost the album's sales. In 2001, she discovered a little more of what she was looking for on Moulin Rouge's soundtrack! Pink collaborated on a soulful remake of Patti LaBelle's "Lady Marmalade" with Christina Aguilera, Mya, and Lil' Kim. Pink released her song Get the Party Started, a total hit from her second album in the same year and went up into the Top 5. It was the ideal launch for M! ssundaztood, her sophomore album, a rock-infused record later on the market, and over 10 million copies world-wide are sold. Pink's third album, Try This, was released in 2003 and earned the singer a hit single ("Trouble") and a Grammy nomination for Best Female Rock Vocal Performance. Despite its critical acclaim, the album did not receive the same recognition or sales level as its predecessor. Pink's fourth album, I'm Not Dead, was released in 2006, and it seemed to be her most honest collection of songs to date. Her album's No. 1 hit single titled Stupid Girls was a pointed assault on people's infatuation and fame like Paris Hilton and Britney Spears. Pink released her compilation album Greatest Hits in 2010, in which her top hit songs F*ckin' Perfect and Raise Your Glass was included. Her subsequent tour was the third most successful in 2013, grossing nearly $148 million in ticket sales. Pink found time outside of her well-known stage name to experiment with other forms of speech. She wrote songs for other artists, such as in Celine Dion's album Closer to the Truth and Cher's album Closer to the Truth. Thanks for Sharing; she co-starred with Mark Ruffalo and Gwyneth Paltrow as a sex addict and earned her critical acclaim in 2013. She's also taken time to explore her more folky side, collaborating with musician Dallas Green on the chart-topping folk album Rose Ave. under the moniker You+Me. In August 2017, Pink released a new song titled What About Us. Beautiful Trauma, her seventh studio album, debuted number one on the Billboard 200 in October with this song as the lead track. In 2018, the pop star showcased her talent at the Grammy Awards in late January and was chosen to sing the national anthem at Super Bowl LII only a few days later her performance in the Grammy's. Pink's eighth studio album, Hurts 2B Human, was released in April 2019 and was the third in a row to top the Billboard 200. Hurts 2B Human included the lead single "Walk Me Home" and collaboration with R&B singer Khalid on the title track, which received positive reviews.

PINK'S FRIENDS AND FOES

 As she is widely open regarding her political views, she publicly tweeted towards President Trump. She will also openly speak out against prominent men like Harvey Weinstein and producer Dr. Luke, who are allegedly got an accusation of sexual harassment and verbal abuse, to demonstrate her support for the women they have abused.

ACCORDING TO KELLY CLARKSON, Pink is the relatable celebrity she will hang out with. They have been performing together and bonding over their talent rather than their appearance to demonstrate their relationship. Pink has friendships with Katy Perry and Hugh Jackman, as shown by her performance in Sydney, Australia. Selma Blair revealed her intimate relationship with Pink, saying that Pink is her "inspiration for joy daily."

. . .

PINK HAS RECEIVED three Grammy Awards in her career. After a couple of years, she won the Best Female Rock Vocal Performance award for her song titled Trouble. She collaborated with Seal, Jeff Beck, and other artists to produce a cover of John Lennon's hit song Imagine in 2011 garnered another Grammy for Best Pop Collaboration with Vocals.

FUN FACTS ABOUT PINK

Here's an exciting truth. Pink has over 20 tattoos, including two of her deceased pets. Her husband is a retired motocross champion, and she has immersed herself in the sport and turned it into something the whole family will enjoy. Another fun fact about her is that she was the one who initiated to propose to her husband after dating for four years.

HOW THE WORLD SEES PINK

She has influenced many who have come into contact with her music since the early 2000s. Pink has a raw edge that acts as motivation and advice to people worldwide. In several of her award ceremonies speeches, she tries to set an example for her daughter by openly discussing her disdain for politics and encouraging every woman in the world. Many people were motivated by her, and she urged everyone to be honest with themselves. Pink is known for her fashion sense, which has included "adventurous" hairstyles, including neon spikes, pink-streaked dreadlocks, and a pitch-black skater cut, in addition to her music. Pink was honored last February of 2019 when she finally received a star on the famous Hollywood Walk of Fame. That same year, she got the title of the People's Champion in 2019 at the People's Choice Awards. After accepting the award, she encouraged the audience to go on and create a change by saying, "Kindness today is an act of rebellion."

. . .

T-MOBILE, V8 supercars, Sony Ericsson, and others are among her other sources of revenue. Pink has worked with CoverGirl, who made her a spokesmodel and featured her in a "beauty with an edge" ad campaign.

"I'm diverse," she told InStyle of her style. I'm a tomboy, but I'm also a hippie and a gangster, which I'm not sure is a good thing, but it's who I am. Pink is also an outspoken supporter of LGBT rights and same-sex marriage. Pink also told The Advocate that she "never felt the need to" describe her sexual orientation. In one of her first interviews, Pink said she didn't want to be one of those singers who sang about things they didn't understand. Her Vietnam veteran father instilled a deep sense of political activism in her.

DESPITE HER RUGGED GIRL APPEARANCE, Pink has shown her caring and compassionate side towards the public. She is one of the women that is a strong advocate for the LGBTQ community and supports the improvement of animal welfare, lending her fame for PETA's campaigns (PETA). She opposed the Australian wool industry's mulesing in collaboration with PETA. In January 2007, she said that PETA misled her about mulesing and did not do enough research before supporting the campaign. Her advocacy culminated last August 21, 2007, in a headlining concert called PAW or Party for Animals Worldwide, held in Cardiff, Wales. In 2015, she went naked for PETA's "I'd Rather Go Naked Than Wear Fur" campaign. The Human Rights Movement, UNICEF, and Save the Children are among the organizations she supports. Since May 2008, Pink has been regarded as an official RSPCA advocate in Australia. On

February 16, 2009, Pink announced that she would contribute $250,000 to the Red Cross Bushfire Appeal for the sake of assisting financial aid on victims of the bushfires that devastated Victoria, Australia, earlier that month. Pink expressed her desire to render "a concrete gesture of encouragement." Pink has donated to the Autism Speaks organization. In 2020 when the coronavirus was widely spreading, she and his son Jameson became positive for this virus which brought them a scare. Following their recovery, the artist revealed that she would donate $1 million to healthcare workers who selflessly risk their lives to ensure care for others during the pandemic. Her mother served as a nurse at the Temple University Hospital in Philadelphia for nearly two decades, and she recently contributed $500,000 to the Mayor's Emergency COVID-19 Crisis Fund in Los Angeles.

FROM HER EDGY music to her fierce beauty, Pink impresses and inspires the world with her message regarding woman empowerment and breaking down discrimination barriers. Pink fully supported the rise of feminism in her way, redefining what a pop star should be and what she should sing about, showing that nobody should tell women who they should be or who they want to be. Pink has challenged gender stereotypes, beauty norms, and femininity since her career. She continues to promote the feminist movement's central message of women standing up to oppression and speaking up to those in positions of authority. Years later, she has kept her promise, singing about personal experiences and real-life problems to send a message to the world that has the potential to change the world.

REFERENCES:

Https://en.wikipedia.org/wiki/Pink_(singer)

https://pink.fandom.com/wiki/I_Have_Seen_the_Rain

https://www.biography.com/musician/pink

https://www.thefamouspeople.com/profiles/pnk-6217.php

https://www.notablebiographies.com/newsmakers2/2004-Ko-Pr/Pink.html

https://www.imdb.com/name/nm0600877/bio

https://www.simplemost.com/pink-facts-singer/

https://esme.com/single-moms/solo-mom-in-the-spotlight/singer-pink-finds-joy-in-here-and-now

https://www.today.com/popculture/pink-performs-after-hospitalization-friends-katy-perry-hugh-jackman-show-t135493

https://www.inquisitr.com/5847400/kelly-clarkson-pink-bond/

https://www.today.com/popculture/kelly-clarkson-pink-relatable-celeb-i-would-actually-hang-t141615

https://www.dailymail.co.uk/tvshowbiz/article-7078327/Selma-Blair-reveals-close-friendship-singer-Pink.html

https://studybreaks.com/culture/music/pink/

https://www.thelist.com/108455/untold-truth-pink/?utm_-campaign=clip

http://www.bornrich.com/pink-singer.html

https://www.popsugar.com/celebrity/photo-gallery/44884682/image/44884697/Carey-Hart

https://gametime.co/blog/what-is-pinks-real-name-inter-esting-facts-about-the-iconic-singer-pink

https://www.allmusic.com/artist/p%21nk-mn0001878899/biography

https://www.hellomagazine.com/profiles/pink/

Photo Credits

Printed in Great Britain
by Amazon

43317330R00030